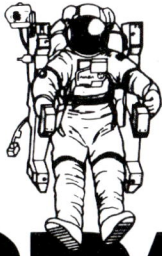

# Space Scientist

# SPACEPROBES
## AND SATELLITES

## Heather Couper and Nigel Henbest

## Franklin Watts
### London   New York   Toronto   Sydney

© 1987 Franklin Watts

First published in 1987 by
Franklin Watts
12a Golden Square
London W1R 4BA

First published in the USA
by Franklin Watts Inc.
387 Park Avenue South
New York, N.Y. 10016

First published in Australia
by Franklin Watts
Australia
14 Mars Road
Lane Cove, NSW 2066

UK ISBN: 0 86313 528 5
US ISBN: 0-531-10360-9
Library of Congress
Catalog Card No:
86-51414

Illustrations by
Drawing Attention
Rhoda Burns
Rob Burns
Eagle Artists
Michael Roffe

Photographs by
British Aerospace
Camera Press
ESA
Mat Irvine
NASA
Novosti Press Agency

Designed by
David Jefferis

Printed in Belgium

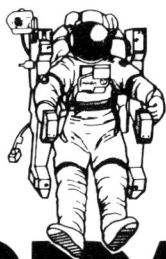

# Space Scientist

# SPACEPROBES
## AND SATELLITES

# Contents

# Exploring space

The whole course of human history changed in the year 1957. Up until then, mankind was bound to the surface of the Earth — and the Earth is just one tiny planet in a vast cosmos.

But on 4 October 1957 a rocket put the first satellite — Sputnik 1 — into orbit around the Earth. Only 15 months later another craft, Luna 1, broke free from the Earth's gravity altogether and plunged into the depths of space. On 12 April 1961 the first human being left the Earth to venture into space; and just over eight years later, men were walking on the Moon.

Although exciting events like these have made the headlines, they are only part of the story of our conquest of space. Space scientists and engineers have followed each new breakthrough with other spacecraft: some have carried people on board; others have been unmanned.

So far, 200 people from 18 countries have been into space. There are literally thousands of unmanned satellites circling the Earth. And over 100 unmanned spaceprobes have gone to the Moon and the other planets.

Space scientists call any object sent intentionally into space a spacecraft. But there *is* a difference between a spaceprobe and a satellite. A spaceprobe is launched at such a speed that it breaks free from the Earth's gravity. A satellite, on the other hand, is launched at a lower speed, so that it goes into an orbit around the Earth. A satellite always feels the pull of the Earth's gravity, but it has enough speed "sideways" that it never falls to the ground — just as you can support a conker on a string as long as you whirl it around fast enough. Unlike a spaceprobe, a satellite is a constant companion of the Earth.

Polar orbit

Equatorial orbit

Venus

Mercury

Sun

Earth

Mars

Jupiter

Saturn

Uranus

△ The spaceprobe Voyager 2 hurtles past the distant planet Uranus and its moons in January 1986. It worked perfectly, even after 8½ years in space.

▷ Satellites (top) always go around the Earth. Spaceprobes (below) escape from the Earth altogether, and they can reach the other planets.

The spaceprobes and some of the satellites orbiting the Earth are designed for purely scientific purposes, to help us understand the Universe and the laws that govern it.

But most satellites are in orbit to benefit mankind and improve human life. If you telephone a country on the opposite side of the world, for example, your call will almost certainly travel via at least one satellite. And we are now used to seeing satellite pictures on television weather forecasts.

Our exploration of space is rather similar to Christopher Columbus's voyages some 500 years ago, when he found the New World. But today's space "ships" are rather different. Satellites are providing services that have become part of our everyday lives, while the spaceprobes are exploring the Solar System and investigating what are literally new worlds!

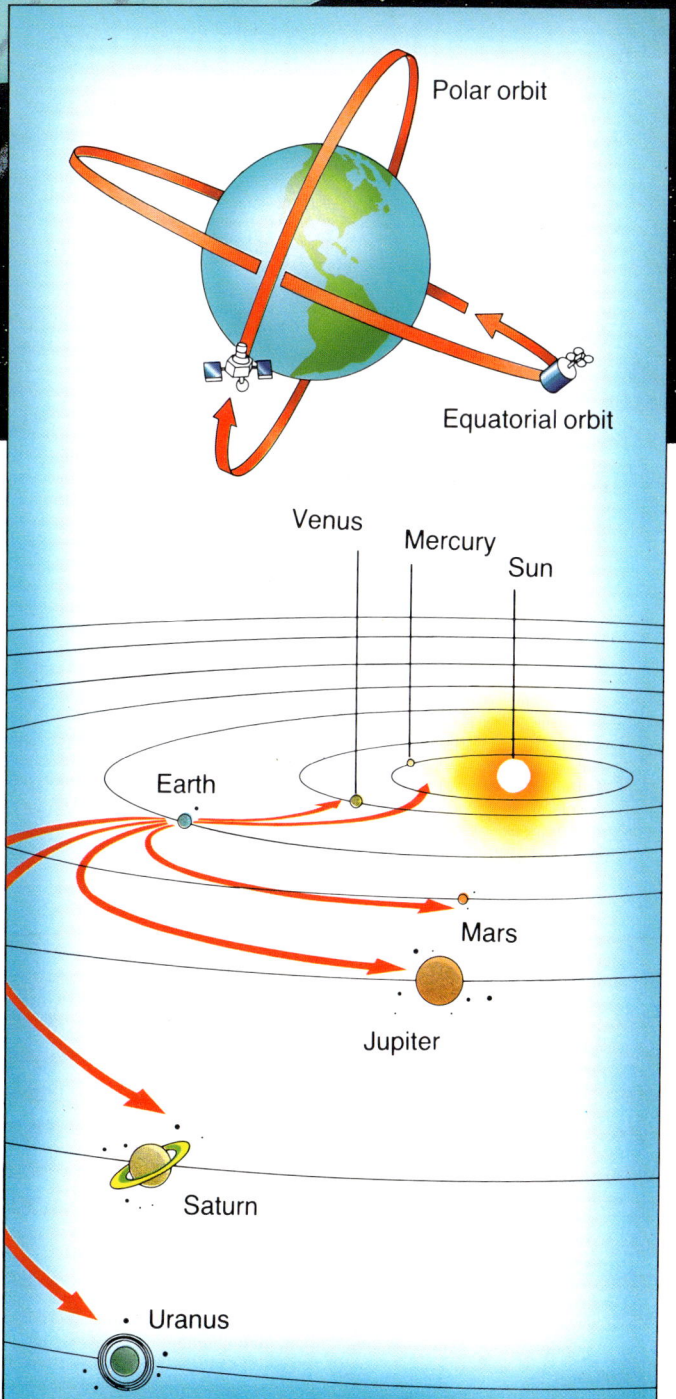

# Into orbit

At first sight, various spacecraft look very different, but they have many family resemblances.

Every spacecraft has a power supply to generate electricity. Most spacecraft use solar cells to turn sunlight into electricity. These cells are either wrapped around the craft or are carried on panels, like huge wings. But a spacecraft travelling a long way from the Sun, like the Voyagers, must generate electricity from a miniature nuclear power station instead.

All satellites and spaceprobes carry both a radio antenna and a computer "brain". These allow people on the ground to contact the spacecraft, sending up instructions and receiving information and pictures in return.

Left to itself, a spacecraft would tumble over and over, so all spacecraft have some kind of stabilization. If an elongated satellite is orbiting the Earth in a vertical position, then the Earth's gravity will keep it this way. Other spacecraft spin around to keep pointing in a constant direction, rather like a gyroscope. The Giotto spaceprobe to Halley's Comet, for example, was spinning fifteen times per minute.

The biggest and most expensive spacecraft, like Voyager, have three-axis stabilization. Jets of gas stop any wobbling or tumbling.

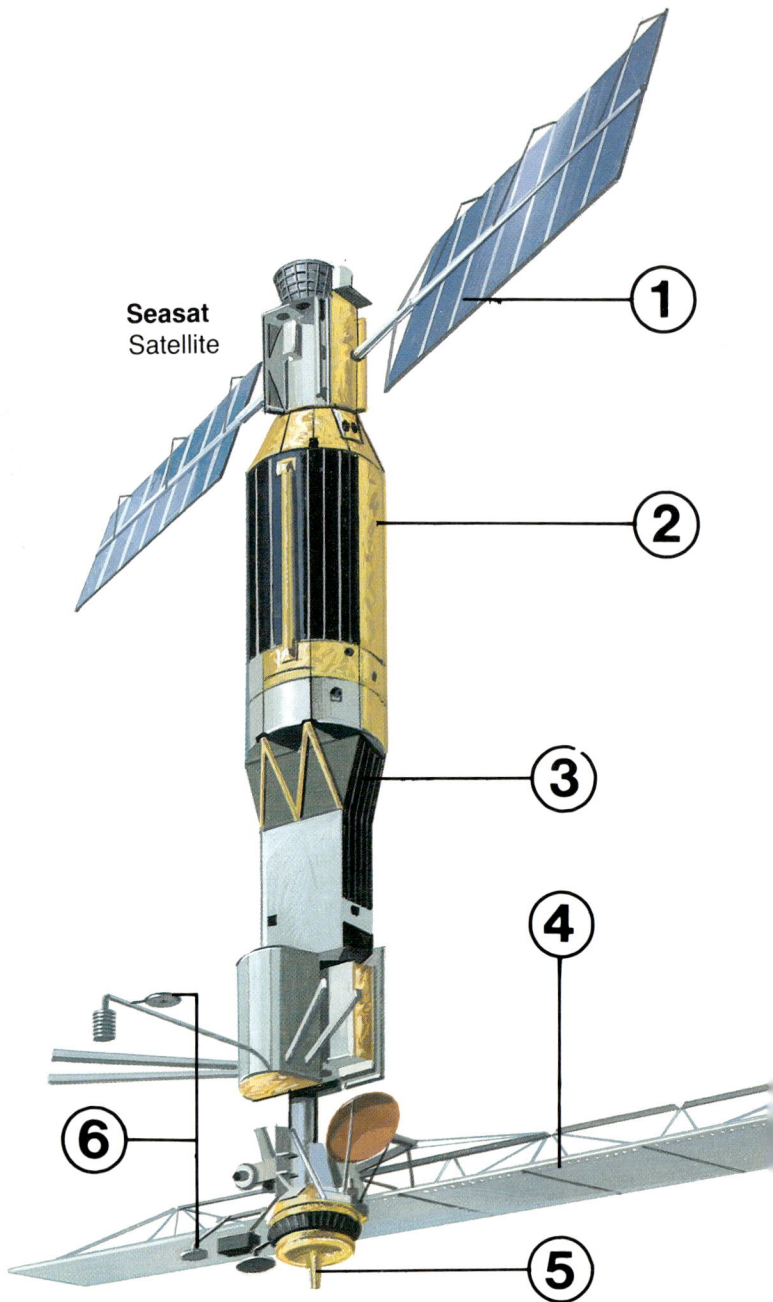

**Seasat** Satellite

① ② ③ ④ ⑥ ⑤

▷ Powerful rockets are needed to launch spacecraft against the pull of Earth's gravity. The US has the Space Shuttle, which carries spacecraft in its cargo bay and can be used many times over, and ordinary rockets like the Titan 4. The European Ariane is designed to put satellites in orbit; it also launched the Giotto probe to Halley's Comet. India and China are now building rockets, too: the Indian PSLV will launch satellites that go over the Earth's poles.

Space Shuttle (USA)

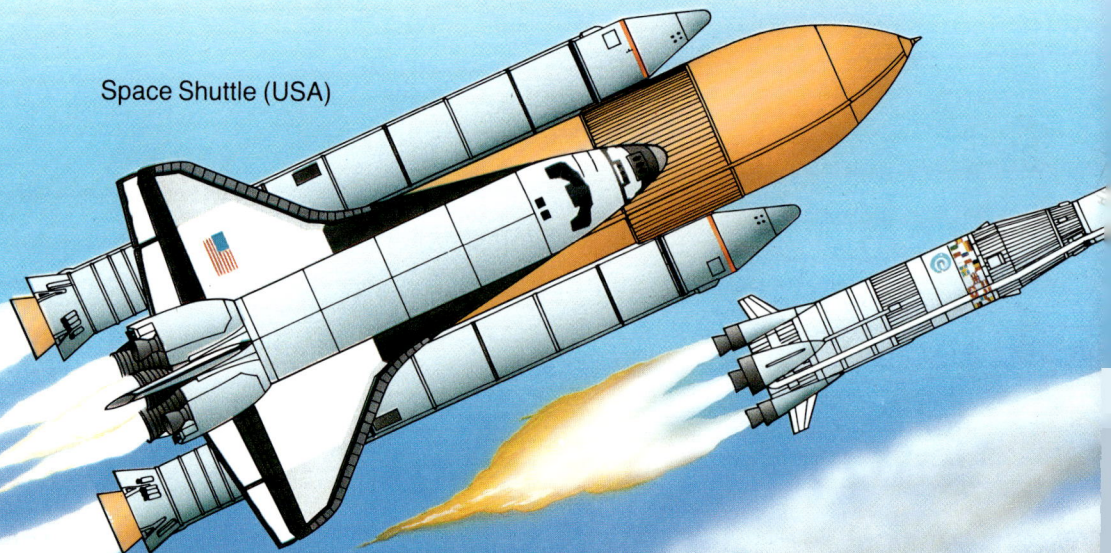

◁ From its orbit above the Earth, Seasat studied the oceans.
**1** Solar panels provide the power supply.
**2** Agena rocket gives the satellite an elongated shape that provides stabilization and keeps Seasat permanently pointing towards the Earth.
**3** Electronics, covered by foil, provide Seasat's computer "brain".
**4** Large panels provide radar "pictures" of the oceans.
**5** Altimeter measures height of the tides below.
**6** Small radio antenna for communicating with the Earth.

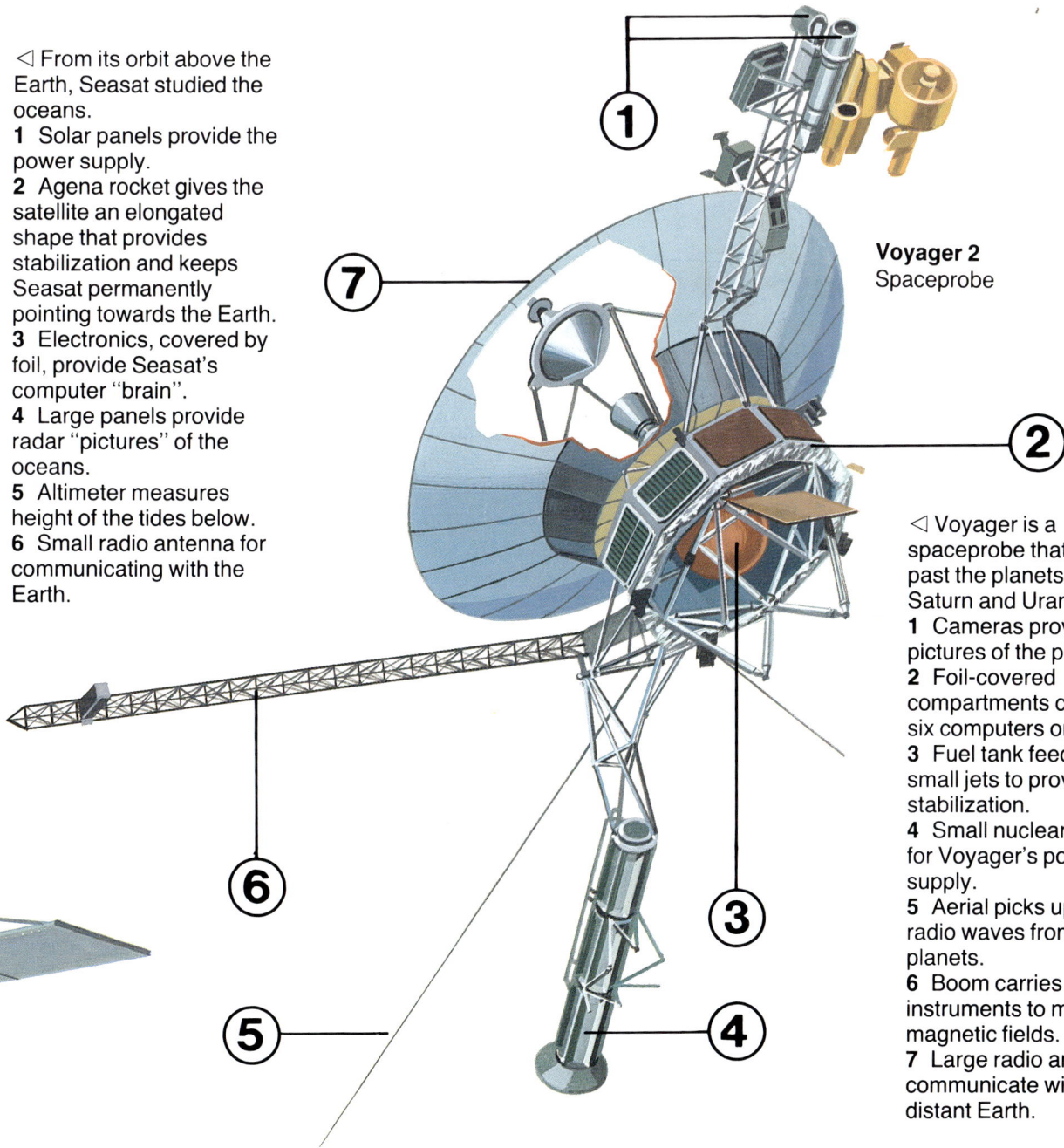

**Voyager 2**
Spaceprobe

◁ Voyager is a spaceprobe that has flown past the planets Jupiter, Saturn and Uranus.
**1** Cameras provide pictures of the planets.
**2** Foil-covered compartments cover the six computers on board.
**3** Fuel tank feeds gas to small jets to provide stabilization.
**4** Small nuclear generator for Voyager's power supply.
**5** Aerial picks up natural radio waves from the planets.
**6** Boom carries instruments to measure magnetic fields.
**7** Large radio antenna to communicate with the distant Earth.

Ariane (Europe)

Titan 4 (USA)

PSLV (India)

Long March (China)

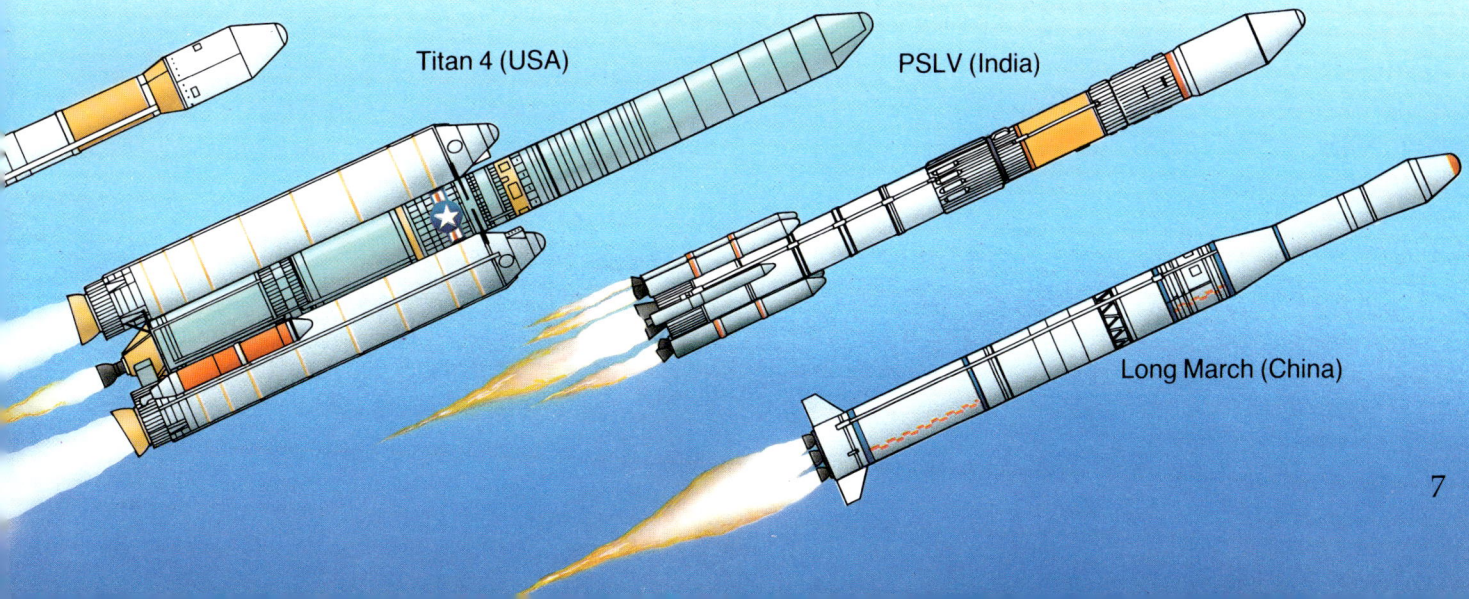

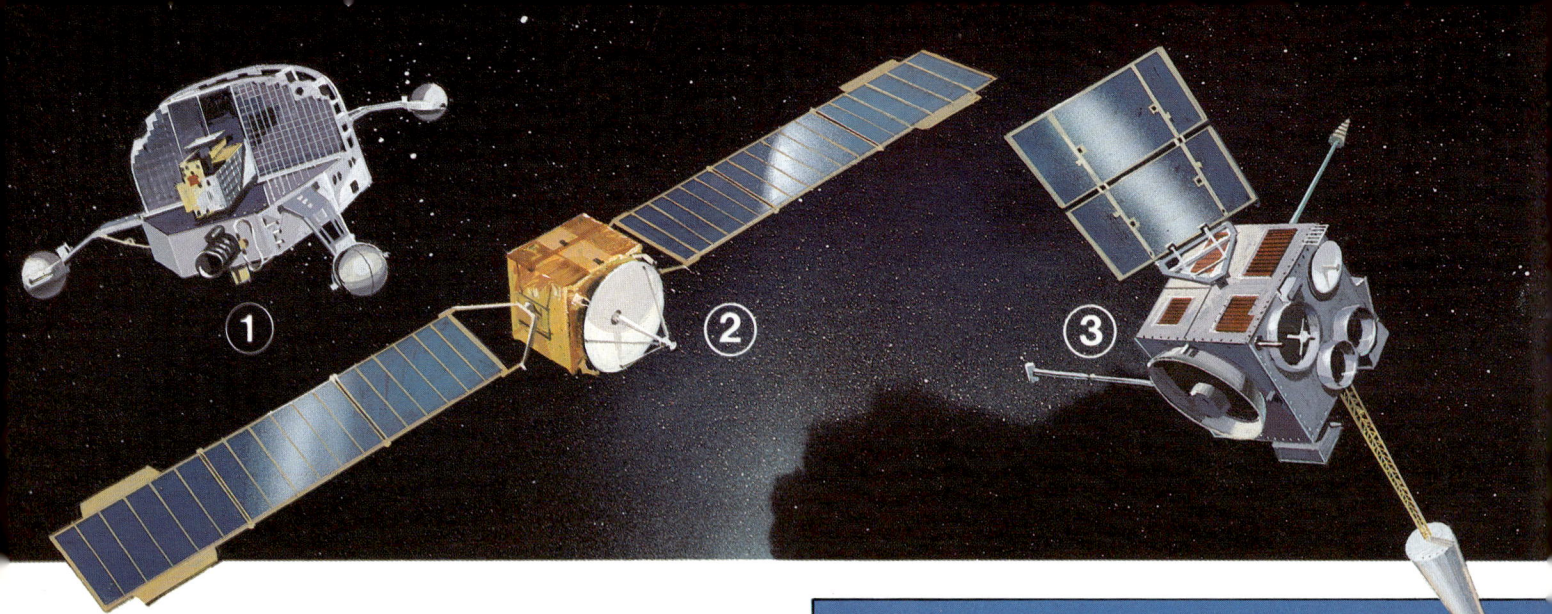

# Using satellites

Since the Soviet Union launched Sputnik 1 in 1957, about 3,000 satellites have been put into different orbits around the Earth. We use them for many different purposes.

The most important satellites in our everyday lives are the communications satellites. We can send radio signals around the world by beaming them up to a communications satellite, which then sends them down to another ground station. Most international phone calls are now sent in this way.

Many television broadcasts now come by satellite. They started with important events like the Olympic Games, but now news reports from around the world are regularly sent by satellite too.

Some satellites are so powerful that you don't need a huge radio antenna to pick up their signals. These "direct broadcast" satellites transmit television programmes that you can receive with a small dish in your own back garden. In a few years you will be able to pick up a huge selection of television programmes from various satellites sent out by several different countries.

Most communications satellites are in large orbits 35,880 km (22,300 miles) above the Earth's equator. There is a particular reason for choosing this orbit, which is known as a geostationary orbit. The time it takes a satellite to go around the Earth depends on how far out it is, getting longer for more distant orbits.

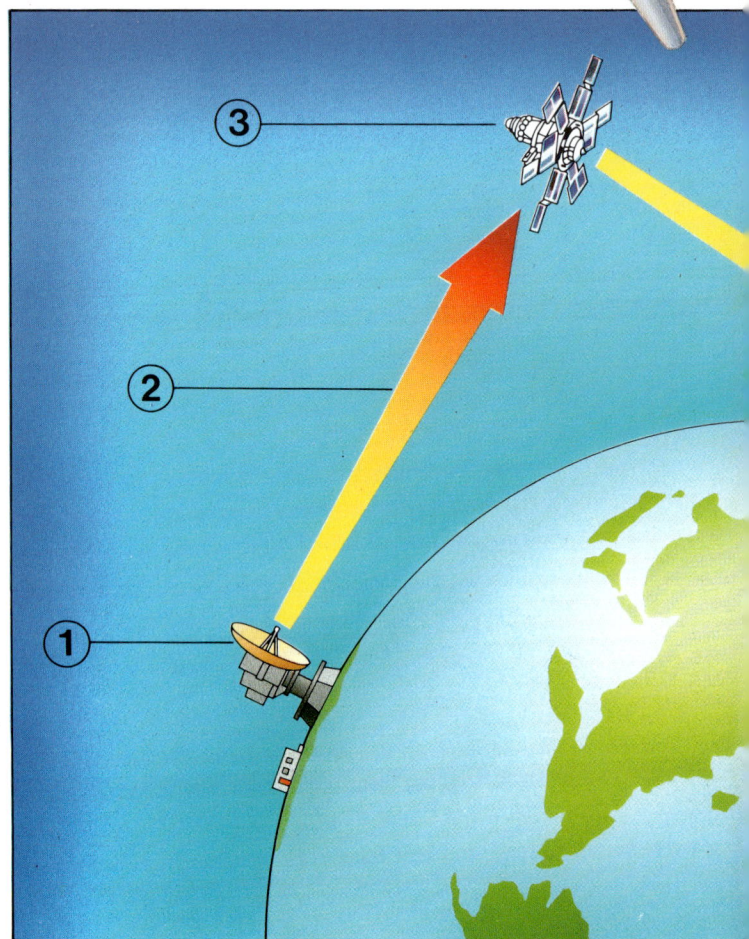

If the satellite is 35,880 km from the Earth, it travels around once in 24 hours and it then appears to "hover" in the same spot over the equator. This makes it easier to design aerials to communicate with the satellite, because they can be fixed to point at just that spot in the sky, rather than having to swing round.

Satellites can also help people on Earth. By picking up the radio signals from navigation satellites, you can find your position on the Earth to the nearest 100 m (300 ft). Search and rescue satellites work the other way round.

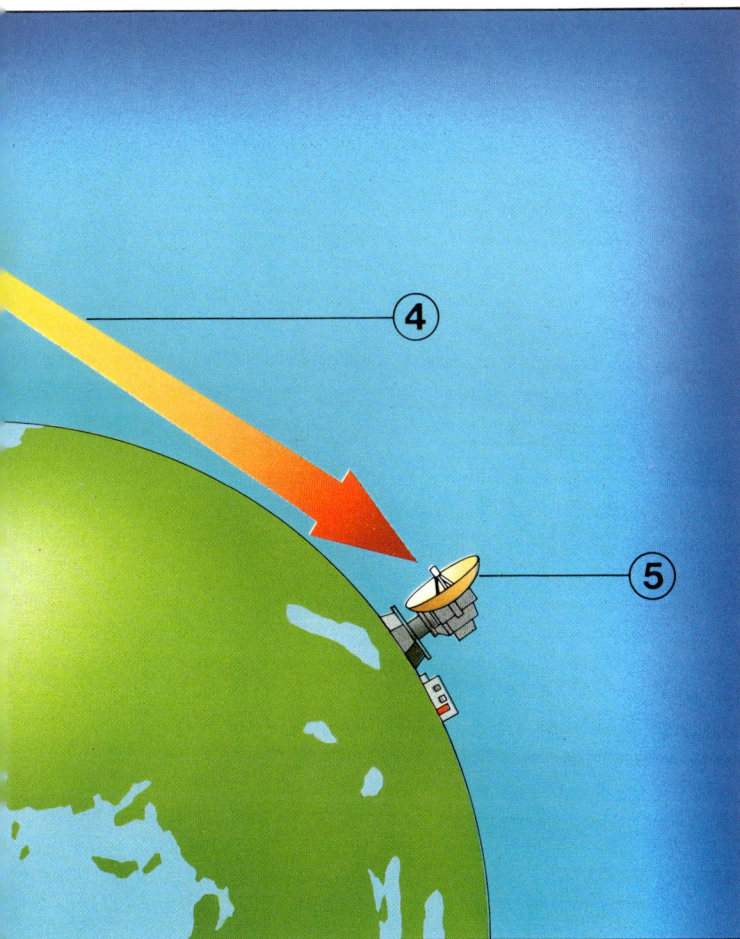

△ Communicating by satellite. The transmitting ground station (**1**) sends a radio message (**2**) to the communications satellite (**3**). The kind shown here is a Soviet Molniya. (The Molniyas are not in geostationary orbits over the equator but are in high orbits over the Soviet Union.) The satellite amplifies the signal, and sends it down (**4**) to a receiving station (**5**).

△ **1** Orbiting Solar Observatory studied radiation from the Sun.
**2** Marecs provides radio links with ships.
**3** GOES 1 watched the weather in North America.
**4** Comstar was a communications satellite.
**5** Meteosat is the weather satellite for Europe.
**6** Advanced Tiros N studies the Earth in radio waves, infrared, ultraviolet and visible light.

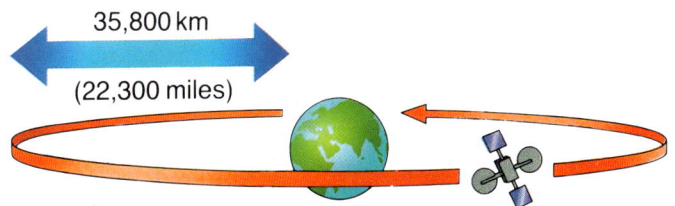

35,800 km
(22,300 miles)

△ **Geostationary orbit** The Earth turns around once every 24 hours. If a satellite is in an orbit with a period of 24 hours, it is going round at the same rate as the Earth. From space, the satellite appears to be on the end of an invisible spoke, always above the same spot on the rotating Earth.

They carry receivers which pick up distress signals from crashed planes or sinking ships, so that rescue teams on the Earth can work out where the calamity has occurred.

A few satellites take no interest in our planet: they look outwards to the distant Universe, to pick up radiations that cannot reach the Earth's surface.

Sad to say, over half the satellites in space are there for military purposes: each week sees the launch of at least two military satellites. Most of them are spy satellites, which take detailed pictures of the Earth; some are for sending radio messages to troops or to navy ships around the world; others are for spying out flashes of radiation from atomic explosions on the Earth.

There are also "killer satellites" that can track down and destroy enemy satellites in time of war. The United States is planning to take this to its extreme with the Star Wars programme (properly known as the Strategic Defence Initiative), in which satellites will shoot down missiles armed with nuclear warheads as they are launched by the enemy.

# Viewing Planet Earth

The cameras aboard a satellite can show us the whole Earth floating in space — putting it into context as just one of the Sun's planets. But satellite pictures have very important practical uses too. From its high position, a satellite can see what's happening anywhere on the Earth below.

A few of the satellites that survey the Earth are in geostationary orbits. Because the satellite always appears to hang over the same point on the Earth (see page 9), it can keep a continuous watch on the same part of the Earth. But the satellite is so far out that its cameras cannot make out small details on the Earth's surface. For this reason, most Earth-observing satellites are in orbits much closer to the Earth. They travel in orbits that go over the Earth's poles, so that successive orbits take them over the entire surface of the Earth.

Weather satellites are among the the most important. From orbit, a satellite can easily see the clouds below. The pictures show how the clouds move, so we can predict the weather for several days ahead. Such accurate forecasts are vital to farmers: they mean that farmers can leave their crops to ripen for the longest possible period, and then harvest them before rain and high winds move in.

Satellites can also show how a hurricane is growing, and so provide a warning that enables the authorities to evacuate people from regions that are threatened. The cost of weather satellites has already been recouped many times over by the amount of money saved by forecasts for farmers and hurricane warnings.

Earth resources satellites are fitted with cameras that "see" not only ordinary light, but also infrared rays from the Earth's surface.

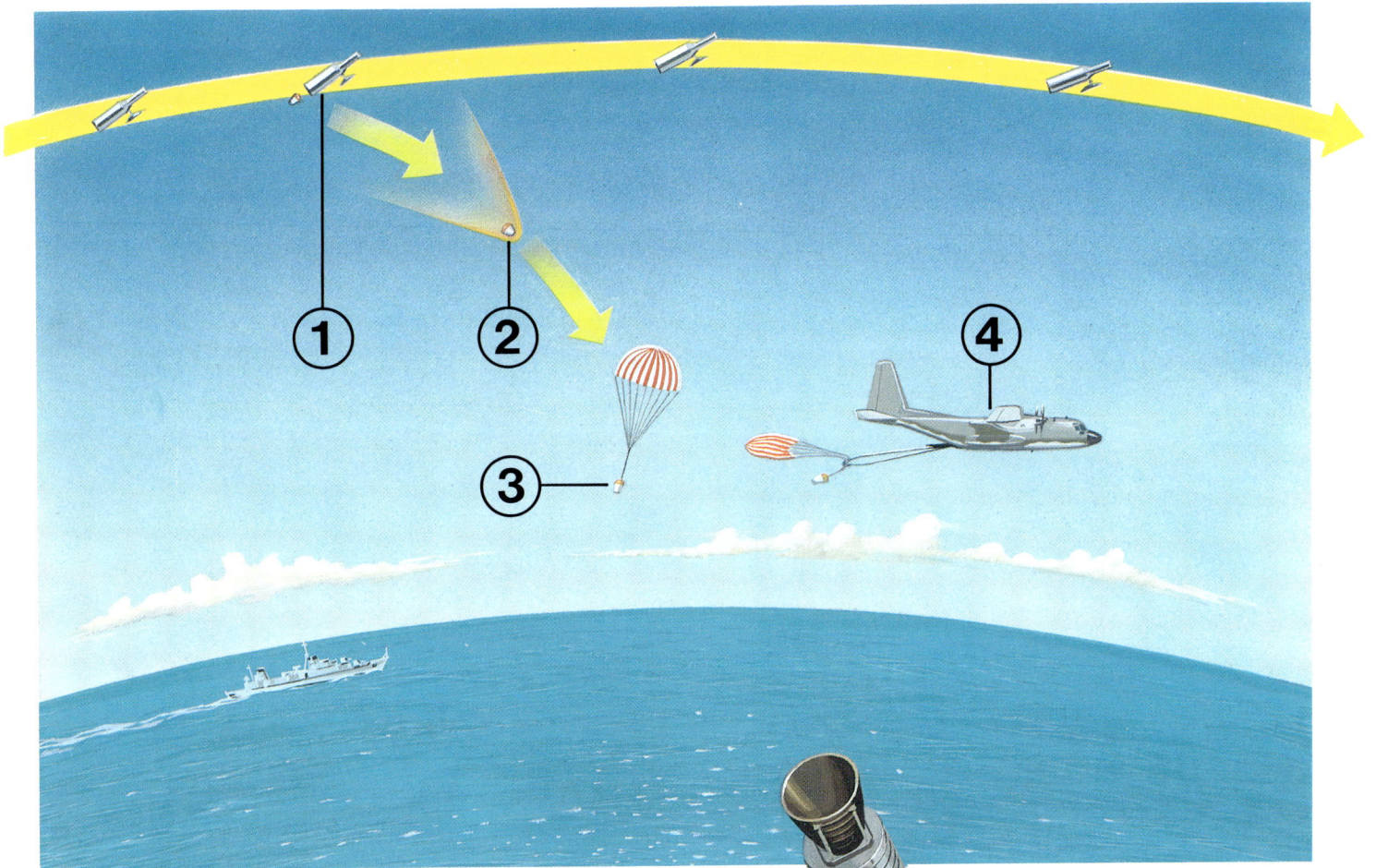

△ How a spy satellite returns its pictures to the Earth. A Big Bird satellite releases a film capsule (**1**). As it enters the Earth's atmosphere (**2**), the capsule glows red hot. Lower in the atmosphere (**3**), a parachute opens. It is caught by a large wire loop trailing behind a C130 military transport plane (**4**).

These satellites allow scientists to pick out the Earth's resources of oil or valuable minerals, for example. The clues come from various tell-tale signs in the surface rocks, revealed by the satellite's high-flying cameras.

As Earth resources satellites pass over the same part of the Earth, day in and day out, they also show how things are changing. So they can reveal places where crops are being destroyed by disease, and show how manmade pollution is spreading out into the oceans.

The original Earth resource satellites, the Landsats, could see details as fine as 40 m (130 ft). The more recent French Spot satellite can see even smaller details. But even Spot is outmatched by the military spy satellites. Their cameras can show so much detail that their pictures reveal whether a person on the ground is wearing a military uniform or not!

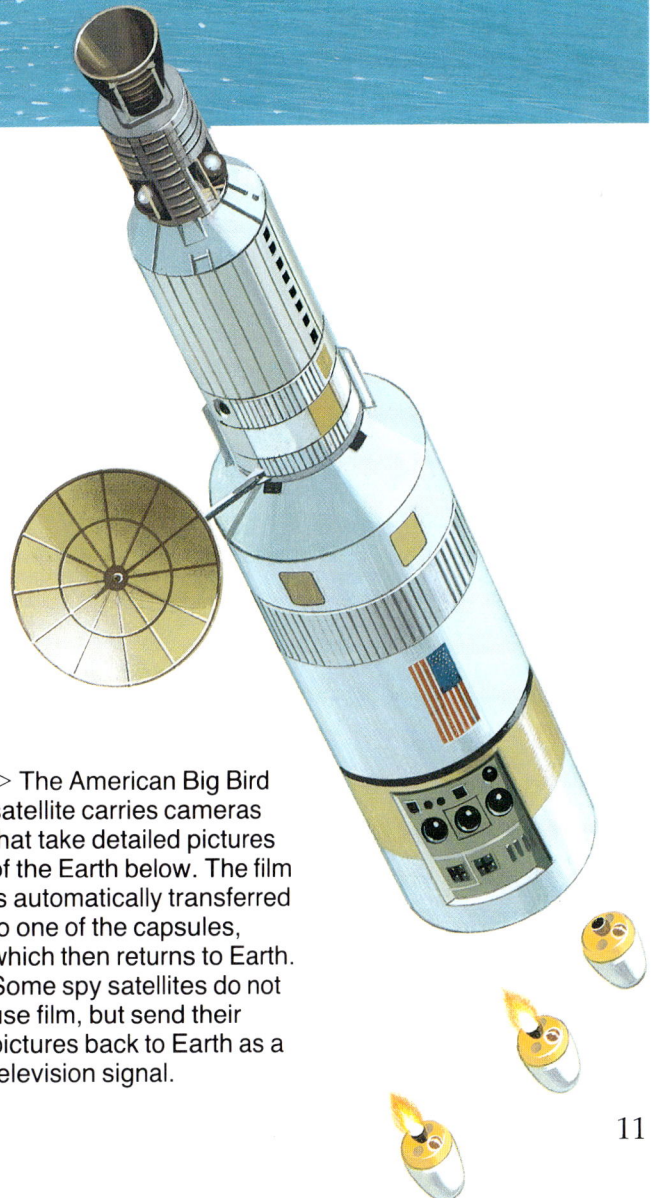

▷ The American Big Bird satellite carries cameras that take detailed pictures of the Earth below. The film is automatically transferred to one of the capsules, which then returns to Earth. Some spy satellites do not use film, but send their pictures back to Earth as a television signal.

# Flying visits

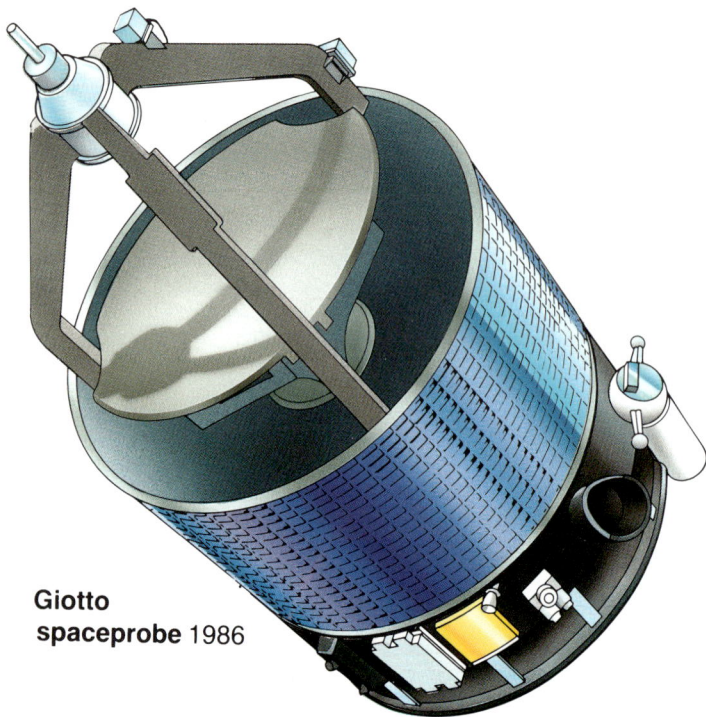

**Giotto spaceprobe** 1986

Our first visits to other worlds have been flying ones. It is difficult to slow down a fast-moving spaceprobe when it reaches its target, so the first spaceprobes to each of the planets have merely shot past, snapping pictures as they hurtled by. In fact, the only pictures we have of Mercury, Jupiter, Saturn and Uranus (and their many moons) have come from flyby probes.

These fleeting glimpses have been enormously valuable. They have shown craters on Mercury, rings around Jupiter, volcanoes on one of Jupiter's moons, millions of thin rings around Saturn, and two dozen new moons.

The Russians took the first pictures of another world from a flyby spaceprobe only two years after they launched the first Earth satellite. In 1959 Luna 3 obtained the first pictures of the far side of the Moon.

The Americans sent the first successful probe past another planet. In 1962 Mariner 2 passed Venus. Although it carried no cameras, its instruments revealed that Venus is baking hot beneath its continuous layer of clouds. Two years later Mariner 4 flew past Mars and sent back pictures of a barren, cratered surface.

In 1974 Mariner 10 became the first spaceprobe to pass two planets. After taking detailed pictures of Venus's clouds, it carried on to fly past Mercury, taking our only close-up pictures of this small, airless, cratered world.

The Americans have also sent the only spaceprobes to venture to the distant giant planets of the Solar System. Pioneers 10 and 11 swept past Jupiter in 1973, with Pioneer 11 going on to Saturn. They were followed by the Voyager 1 and 2 spaceprobes. The Voyager design included better cameras and a "brain" that consisted of six computers linked together. After passing Jupiter, both Voyagers flew on to Saturn, sending back some 70,000 pictures of each world.

Voyager 2 went on to fly past Uranus in 1986, and it is on course to pass its fourth planet, Neptune, in 1989. By then, spaceprobes will have passed all the planets except for Pluto.

When Halley's Comet returned to the Sun in 1986, it was travelling too fast for spacecraft to rendezvous with the comet. So the five probes that went to Halley's Comet had to fly past it — at a speed of 250,000 km/h (155,000 mph)!

**Mariner 10** to Venus and Mercury

**Mars 3** landed a capsule in 1971

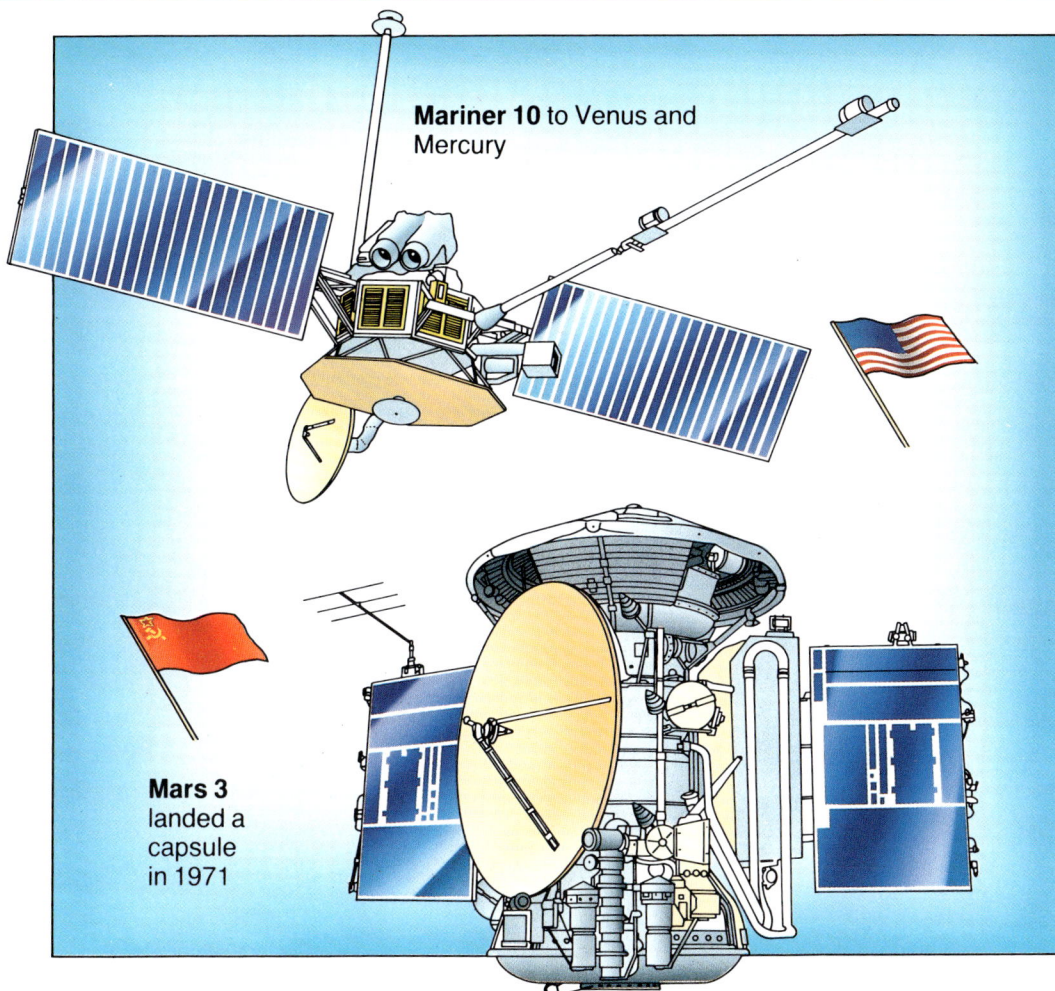

△ The European spaceprobe Giotto took very detailed pictures of the solid dark nucleus at the heart of Halley's Comet. As Giotto flew through the comet in March 1986 at a speed of 250,000 km/h (155,000 mph), small dust particles hit the spaceprobe with enough force to damage it.

◁ Mariner 10 flew past Venus, with its thick poisonous clouds, and airless Mercury. Because the Sun's light is more intense near Venus and Mercury, Mariner 10 needed only two solar panels to generate electricity, rather than the four used on America's spaceprobes to Mars. The Russian Mars 3 spaceprobe ejected a capsule that landed on Mars in 1971, sending back information but no pictures.

# Orbiting other worlds

On 13 November 1971 an American spaceprobe fired its retrorockets, slowing down its breakneck pace past the red planet Mars. As its speed fell away, the probe came under the influence of Mars's gravity, and its path curled round into an orbit around the planet. Mariner 9 had become the first artificial satellite of another planet.

An orbiting spaceprobe can tell us far more about a planet than a flyby mission. A flyby probe can study the planet for only a few days, at best, and it may photograph only part of the planet. An orbiting spaceprobe can see the whole of the planet, and keep it under surveillance for years.

Mariner 9 really showed the value of an orbiter. The previous flyby probes (Mariners 4, 6 and 7) had taken pictures of just one part of Mars, and that was cratered and uninteresting.

When Mariner 9 arrived at Mars, the planet was totally hidden under a great duststorm. A flyby probe would have sent back no useful pictures at all. But eventually the dust settled, and the cameras began to show a whole range of unexpected sights: giant volcanoes and huge canyons — both far larger than any on Earth — and dried-up river beds.

Both the Russians and the Americans have also put spaceprobes into orbit around Venus. The Pioneer Venus probe not only took pictures of Venus's swirling clouds, but used a radar set to probe beneath the clouds and produce the first map of Venus's rocky surface below.

The Russian Venera 15 and 16 probes carried a more sophisticated radar that revealed ridges and rings on Venus's surface. The rings may be old craters, or the stumps of volcanoes worn away by Venus's erosive atmosphere.

◁ The Viking 1 Orbiter about to release a capsule to land on the Red Planet. After the first manmade satellite of Mars, Mariner 9, found dried-up river beds on Mars, two Viking probes were sent to take a closer look. The Viking Orbiters took the first colour pictures of Mars, sent back to Earth by the large antenna.

▷ The hidden surface of Venus, as revealed by the radar set on the Pioneer Venus orbiter. The radio waves used for radar can penetrate the ever-present clouds on Venus — just as radar at an airport can reveal planes hidden by cloud. This contour map shows that most of Venus is a rolling plain. There are some large plateaus and a few high mountains that may be volcanoes.

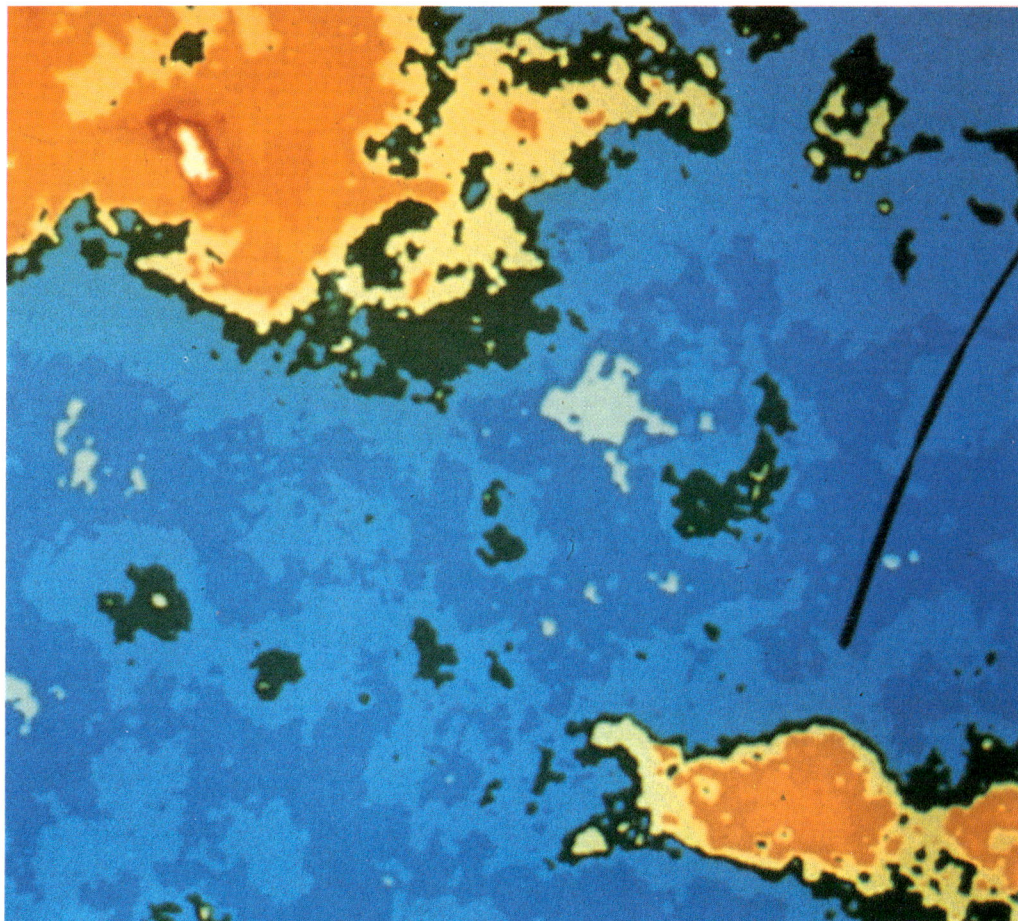

# Touchdown!

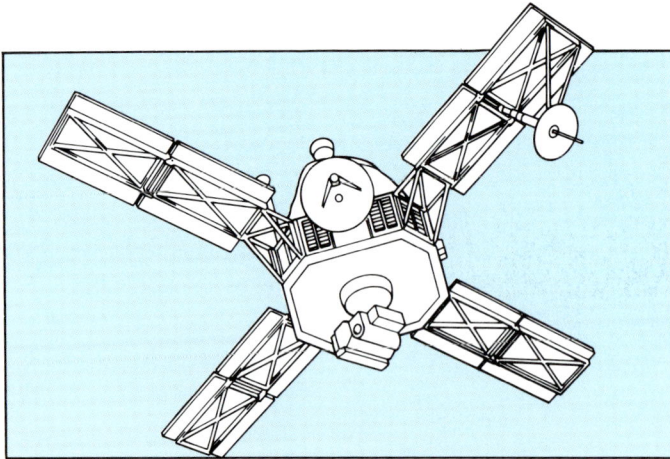

Each Viking started as a lander and an orbiter joined together. After the lander separated (**1**), an aeroshell protected it from overheating as it plunged into Mars's atmosphere (**2**).

It then ejected the aeroshell and deployed a parachute (**3**). When the lander was 1,400 m above the ground, it released the parachute and used rockets to land gently.

By far the best way to explore another world is actually to land on it. So far, astronauts have only reached one other world, the Moon, but unmanned spaceprobes have also landed on the two nearest planets. Purely by historical chance, the Russians are now firmly associated with Venus, and the Americans with the planet Mars.

Venus is a tough problem for any spacecraft designer. Beneath its acid clouds, the pressure increases to 90 times the Earth's atmospheric pressure, and the temperature rises to 475°C (890°F). The first three Russian probes to parachute through Venus's atmosphere were crushed by the pressure before they reached the red-hot surface.

But in 1970 the heavily armoured capsule of Venera 7 landed safely on Venus. In 1975 Veneras 9 and 10 sent back the first pictures of Venus's surface, in black and white. The first colour pictures came from Veneras 13 and 14 in 1982. At all four of these landing sites the cameras revealed bare rocks stretching to the horizon.

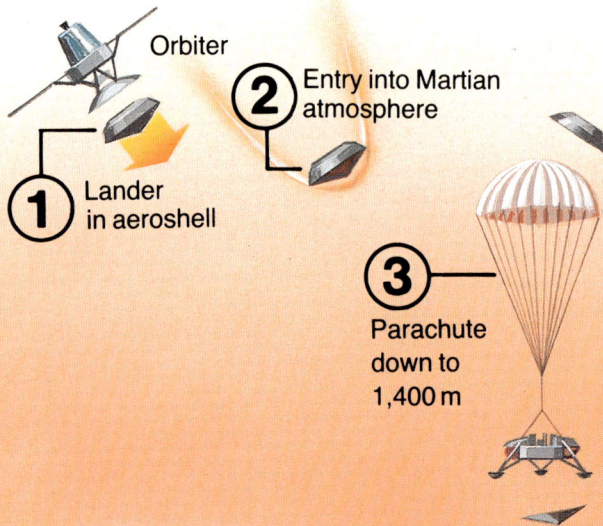

Orbiter

**2** Entry into Martian atmosphere

**1** Lander in aeroshell

**3** Parachute down to 1,400 m

Rocket braking to touchdown

In 1985 two Vega probes passed Venus on their way to Halley's Comet. They dropped off not only a pair of landers but also two balloons. These floated in Venus's clouds for 48 hours, swept along and up-and-down by powerful winds.

The Americans have had a highly successful pair of landers on Mars (where the Russians have had a string of failures). The dried-up river beds of Mars suggested to some scientists that some kind of life might have started up when Mars was wet, even if it was just microscopic cells in the soil. They sent the Viking Landers to look for signs of life.

Each lander carried a miniature laboratory to search for life. Controllers back on the Earth instructed the lander to load some soil into the laboratory, to warm it up and add water. They then investigated whether the soil gave off gases. At first the results looked very encouraging: gas was being released. But it now seems that the gases did not come from living cells, but from a chemical reaction between the soil and the water.

△ The Russian Lunokhod is the only unmanned vehicle to have travelled around on another world: two Lunokhods explored the Moon in the early 1970s. The unmanned landers on the Moon gave both the Russians and the Americans experience in designing landers for the other planets. Future rovers will have computer brains so that they can avoid rocks without having to wait for instructions from Earth.

▽ A Viking Lander touches down on Mars. Its main mission is to search for life, but it will also find out what the soil and atmosphere are made of, and take colour pictures of its surroundings.

17

# Future missions

Although spaceprobes like the Voyagers, the Veneras and the Vikings have been tremendously successful, space scientists are not content with their results.

They have sent probes to the planets to answer some long-standing questions — for example: is there life on Mars, what lies under the clouds of Venus, why does Saturn have rings? But every time a spaceprobe has investigated another planet, it has come up with more new questions than answers!

So space engineers and scientists are now designing new probes to find out even more about the other planets and moons of the Solar System.

The Russians are building a spaceprobe to go into orbit around Mars. This craft, called Phobos, will investigate Mars's larger moon, Phobos, as well as the Red Planet itself.

▷ A Russian spaceprobe moves in towards Mars's larger moon, Phobos, in 1989. The spacecraft, also called Phobos, is shooting a laser beam at the moon to burn off a small amount of its surface. By analyzing the gases, scientists hope to find out what Phobos is made of. A lander in the background "hops" around Phobos taking pictures of its surface.

The Americans have also designed a new spaceprobe to go into orbit around Mars (and one for Venus, as well). For the more distant future they are beginning to plan a new Mars lander, which will have a "rover" that can travel across the red deserts. It will seek out a site for a future manned base on Mars.

Looking to the next planet out, the Americans have built a new Jupiter spaceprobe, Galileo. Rather like the Viking probes to Mars, Galileo has both an orbiter and a probe that will dive into Jupiter's atmosphere (although it cannot "land" because Jupiter has no solid surface). For two years at least, the Galileo Orbiter will watch the swirling clouds of Jupiter, and the eruptions of the volcanoes on its moon Io.

European space scientists are discussing with the Americans a similar mission to the next planet, Saturn. In this spacecraft, called Cassini, the Orbiter will watch the rotation of Saturn's perplexing rings. The atmosphere probe will not be sent to Saturn itself, but to its large moon Titan. Titan has a thick atmosphere with orange clouds which is like the Earth's original atmosphere, preserved in "deep freeze".

The five probes that went to Halley's Comet in 1986 were so successful that cometary scientists are now intent on building a probe to visit another comet.

By choosing a comet that is moving more slowly than Halley's, the mission planners will be able to bring the spaceprobe alongside the solid nucleus at the comet's centre. The probe will then dispatch a lander, which will settle on to the surface of the nucleus, between the jets of gas and dust that erupt from it. The lander will scoop out a piece of the comet, returning it to the orbiter for analysis on Earth.

△ The ringed planet Saturn is the target for a future US-European mission called Cassini, after the astronomer who first studied Saturn's rings. The probe will try to find out why the rings are composed of narrow ringlets and what makes up the orange clouds of Saturn's moon Titan.

# Russians in space

Robot satellites and spaceprobes can do many useful tasks in space, and they have the advantage that they are cheaper than sending up people. We are also not so concerned if the spacecraft fails. But there are some tasks that only humans can perform.

The Russians took the lead in launching "spacemen" — more properly called cosmonauts. On 12 April 1961 a rocket launched Yuri Gagarin into orbit. In his Vostok capsule, Gagarin hurtled once around the Earth.

During the 1960s Gagarin was followed by many other cosmonauts, including the first spacewoman, Valentina Tereshkova. Another Russian, Alexei Leonov, was the first person to float in space outside his spacecraft. But the Russians ran into problems in the late 1960s. The Russians gave up the "space race" after the Americans landed a man on the Moon in 1969.

They then concentrated on putting space stations into orbit around the Earth. A space station is a large spacecraft where people can live for long periods of time. The station itself stays in orbit, and the cosmonauts travel up and down in smaller capsules called Soyuz.

The first five space stations in the Salyut series were not very successful, but Salyut 6 and Salyut 7 became the first true homes in space. In 1986 the Russians launched an improved space station called Mir.

The crews stay on board for several months. During this time supplies of food and fuel are brought up by an unmanned "space ferry" which docks automatically with the space station. The cosmonauts also have visitors, who arrive in a separate Soyuz craft for a week-long visit. The Russians have offered trips to people from a dozen other countries.

△ A Soyuz craft (left) brings a crew to the Mir space station. Visiting spacecraft can dock at either end of Mir. The "wings" are solar panels to provide power. Four extra modules will be permanently attached to Mir to increase its size. Eventually Mir will be permanently manned.

△ Russian cosmonaut Valeriy Bykovsky and an East German guest cosmonaut, Sigmund Jähn, stride through the assembly testing building at the Baikonur space centre. These two cosmonauts flew on the Soyuz 31 mission that visited the Salyut 6 space station in August 1978.

The Russian space stations are designed so that scientists can do experiments that would not be possible on an unmanned satellite.

The cosmonauts have used powerful cameras and telescopes to look both towards the Earth and at distant stars and galaxies.

The space station also gives scientists their only chance to do experiments in weightless conditions. The crew in an orbiting craft are not beyond the range of Earth's gravity, but they feel "weightless" because they are actually orbiting the Earth themselves, and along exactly the same path that the space station is following — so they just float around inside it.

In weightless conditions cosmonauts can make new kinds of materials, by melting substances, mixing them, and letting them cool and solidify. On the Earth gravity usually separates such substances because the heavier one sinks to the bottom of the container. The cosmonauts can also make extremely pure crystals of semiconductors — the material that is used in electronic chips.

The cosmonauts are also investigating how plants and animals grow in weightless conditions. This helps scientist understand how gravity affects living beings.

Just as important is the investigation of the cosmonauts' own bodies — to discover the medical effects of weightlessness. The Russians have found that after a few weeks of weightlessness their muscles wither away, because they are not working against gravity all the time. So the cosmonauts spend hours every day doing exercises. More serious is the fact that weightlessness makes the bones brittle. Until there is a cure, manned flights are limited to less than a year.

# America's space missions

The first American, John Glenn, orbited the Earth almost a year after Gagarin's flight. But in the next 7½ years the Americans not only sent two-man and three-man crews into orbit, but landed a man on the Moon. Between 1969 and 1972 12 astronauts (the American term for a "spaceman") walked on the Moon.

The mid-1970s saw a historic handshake in space, when an Apollo crew linked with a Russian crew in a Soyuz, and America's first space station, Skylab, which was constructed from the top stage of a Saturn rocket.

The United States was by this time working on the Space Shuttle: a rocket that could be used over and over again to transport astronauts and satellites into space simply and cheaply. It consists of an orbiter, which looks rather like a plane, attached to a large fuel tank with two solid-fuel boosters.

The first Shuttle, Columbia, was launched in 1981. It was joined by three others: Challenger, Discovery and Atlantis. Over the next five years they made 24 flights. The Shuttles launched satellites of all kinds. They also carried into orbit Spacelab, a laboratory built by European scientists. On some missions the astronauts went on space walks to repair satellites.

But in January 1986 an explosion destroyed the orbiter Challenger, killing its crew of seven. The tragedy caused a delay of at least two years while problems were sorted out.

The Americans have two major new plans. Star Wars is a system of satellites that is supposed to make the United States safe from nuclear war by shooting down missiles launched from Russia. More peaceful is the Space Station, which will be bigger and better than the Russians', for the mid-1990s.

▷ American astronaut Bruce McCandless was the first person to fly in space as a "human satellite", unattached to a spacecraft. He used rockets in his backpack to fly about.

◁ In the year 2000, spacecraft of many nationalities converge on the American Space Station (top right). Astronauts from the United States arrive in the Space Shuttle (left). After the Shuttle tragedy of 1986, the Americans used ordinary rockets, like the one shown top left, for heavy unmanned loads. European astronauts fly up in the British-built spaceplane Hotol (right). Hotol is a plane when it is in the atmosphere and a rocket in space. A Japanese shuttle (bottom) is filming the activity. The Space Station is partly built by the Europeans, Japanese and Canadians.

# To the stars!

To date over 200 people have travelled into space. Although most of them have only gone into a low orbit around the Earth, 24 astronauts have gone as far as the Moon.

But even so, the Moon is right on our doorstep in space. So when can we expect people to visit the planets?

Venus is out of the question, certainly in the near future — the pressure and temperature are just too high. But there are no practical reasons why people should not land on Mars. The main problem is the long journey time: a round trip would take at least two years.

The Russians may well be planning a Mars expedition. Their long stays on space stations may be to test how the human body will adapt to a trip to Mars — and the Mir space station is an ideal prototype for an interplanetary craft.

Looking even further ahead, people may one day travel to the stars. Indeed, four of our unmanned probes (Pioneers 10 and 11, and Voyagers 1 and 2) are moving so fast that they will break free of the Sun's gravity and end up travelling among the distant stars.

But the immensity of space is a formidable obstacle: it just takes so long to get anywhere. Voyager 2, for example, is travelling so fast that it can reach the edge of the Solar System in only 12 years: but it would take another 80,000 years to reach the nearest star!

Space scientists have thought of two ways to overcome this problem. One is to shorten the journey time, with new, more powerful kinds of rocket. Engineers have already tested an ion drive, in which atoms are torn apart and the fragments (ions) are speeded up by electric fields. Or the spaceship might have no engine at all: instead it would carry a large reflector, and a powerful laser on the Earth would "blow" it away by pressure of its light.

The other answer is to travel fairly slowly and accept the lengthy voyage. We could perhaps keep the crew alive in hibernation. Or we might build a large spaceship that would carry a crew of several hundred. Generations of crew members would live and die over the thousands of years that the ship was under way. It would be the distant descendants of the original crew who would eventually arrive at the target star and explore its planets.

△ The huge Daedalus starship (note the Space Shuttle to scale) would blast its way to the stars. It has two stages, each with a set of round fuel tanks holding billions of miniature hydrogen bombs. These are fed to the big hemispherical combustion chamber, where they explode. The blast from the bombs propels Daedalus forward. This starship could be built early in the next century: it would reach the nearest star in fifty years.

▷ In the distant future a "space ark" — hollowed out of an asteroid — uses the gravity of Saturn to swing it away from the Sun and into deep space. Hundreds of men, women and children live inside the ark. It spins around so that centrifugal force provides artificial gravity. Powerful lamps provide "sunlight" so that plants can grow. Many generations will live and die before the ark reaches its target — a new planetary system which they will colonize.

## Inside the space ark

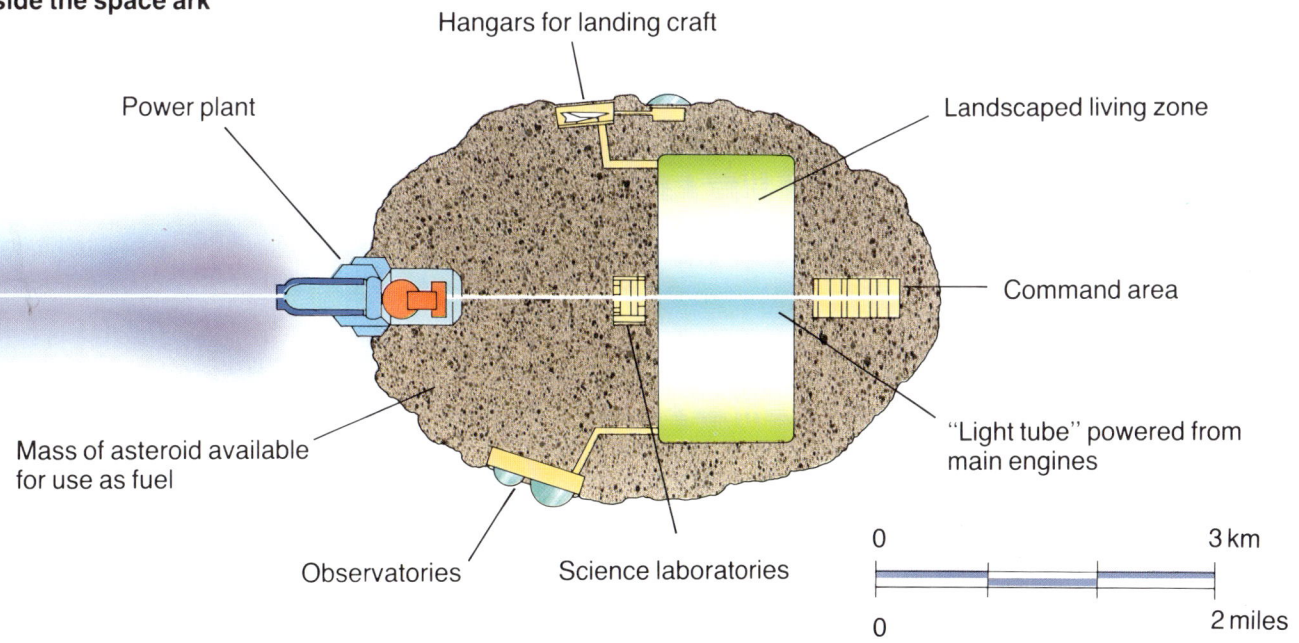

Power plant

Hangars for landing craft

Landscaped living zone

Command area

Mass of asteroid available for use as fuel

"Light tube" powered from main engines

Observatories

Science laboratories

| 0 | | 3 km |
|---|---|---|
| 0 | | 2 miles |

# Spotting satellites

There are dozens of satellites in orbit that are bright enough for you to spot easily with your unaided eye.

A satellite appears as a point of light in the sky and is usually about the same brightness as a star. At first you may mistake it for a star — until you notice that it is moving slowly.

The only thing you could mistake for a satellite is a high-flying plane, but you can usually tell a plane by the sound of its engines. A plane also has red and green lights on its wings. If you can't see these with your naked eye, a pair of binoculars will show them clearly.

Some local papers give predictions of when satellites are visible, so you can find out which one you are looking at.

## When to look

You will only see satellites at certain times each day, during a couple of hours in the morning before dawn and a couple of hours in the evening after sunset.

This is because satellites have no light of their own. We see them because they reflect sunlight. During the day we cannot see satellites against the bright blue sky. In the middle of the night satellites are invisible because they are in eclipse — in the Earth's shadow where no sunlight falls on them.

A satellite will often move into eclipse as you watch it crossing the sky. You will see its brightness fade, until the satellite totally disappears.

Earth's shadow: satellites are invisible when passing through it

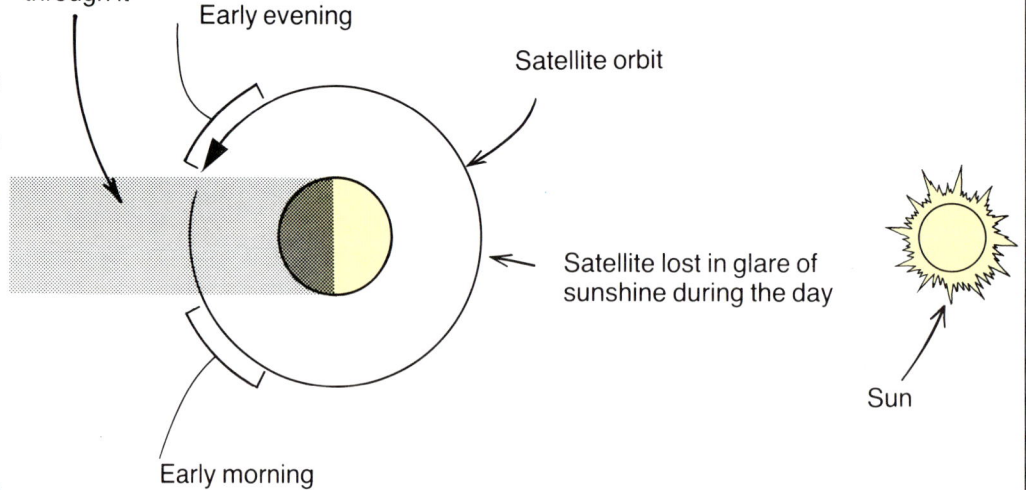

Early evening

Satellite orbit

Satellite lost in glare of sunshine during the day

Sun

Early morning

Not to scale

## Manned vehicles

If you see a very brilliant satellite — brighter than any star — the chances are that it is a manned spacecraft. The American Space Shuttle and the Russian Mir space station are so big that they reflect a lot of sunlight; they also appear bright because they are in low orbits and so are quite close to us.

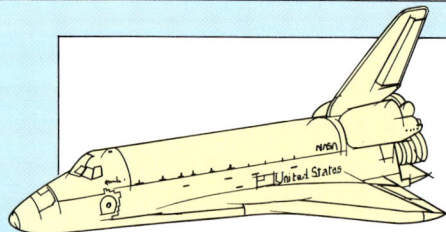

Space Shuttle: flights should resume in 1988

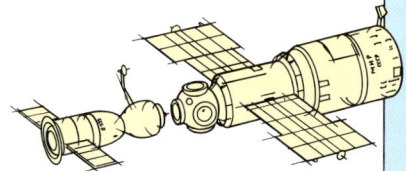

Mir space station: in orbit now

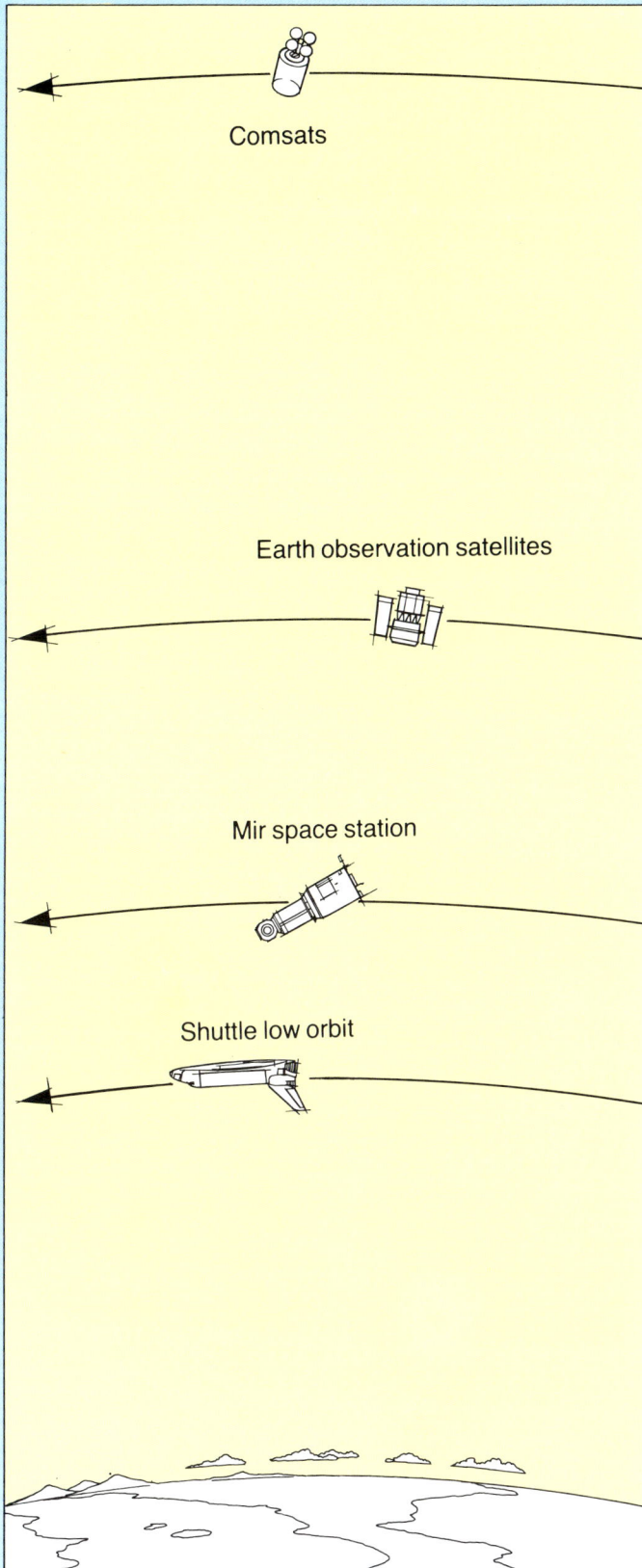

Comsats

Earth observation satellites

Mir space station

Shuttle low orbit

## Orbits

You can tell a satellite's height, roughly, from the speed it crosses the sky. A satellite in a very low orbit (like the Shuttle) goes from horizon to horizon in only five minutes. Higher satellites take longer. A satellite going north-south (or south-north) is in orbit over the poles to study all parts of the Earth's surface: it is a weather, Earth resources or spy satellite.

## Flashing satellites

As different parts of a satellite catch the Sun's light, we see its brightness changing. If a satellite is spinning, it flashes regularly as it crosses the sky. Sometimes you cannot see it at all between the flashes. A satellite with large solar panels does not spin, because the panels must always face the Sun. But the panels occasionally reflect sunlight in our direction, producing a sudden and very bright flash of light. If you see a sudden flash from the northern part of the sky, it is probably caused by a Russian Molniya satellite.

# Spacecraft directory

Satellites and spaceprobes come in all sizes — and almost in all shapes! The first were quite small, but as rocket power increased, so they became larger and heavier: compare the first

Russian and American satellites with the Mir Space Station and the Hubble Space Telescope. These structures in Earth orbit are larger than the probes we can send to the planets.

**Spacecraft to scale:**
**1** Sputnik 1 (1957), first satellite.
**2** Explorer 1 (1958), first US satellite.
**3** Navstar navigation satellite (1978).
**4** Molniya 2 communications satellite (1971).
**5** Hubble Space Telescope (1988?).
**6** Voyager spaceprobe (1977).
**7** Viking Orbiter (Mars, 1976).
**8** Mir space station (1986).

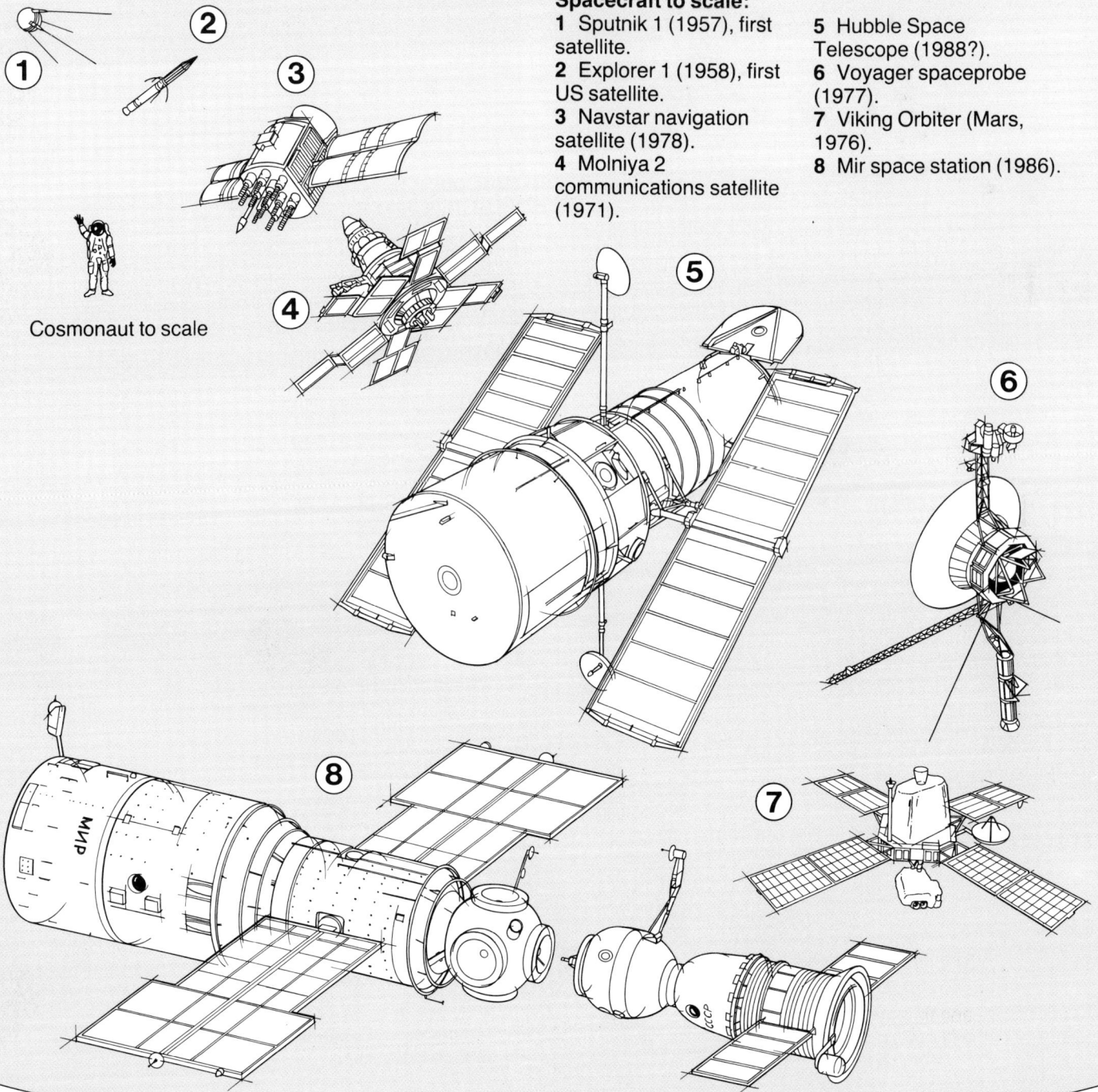

Cosmonaut to scale

# Decoding satellite pictures

You will often find pictures of the Earth taken from space in books, magazines and exhibitions. Some are ordinary photographs, but others use infrared rays, and give a picture in false colours where green vegetation, for example, appears red. The examples below show some of the landmarks to look out for in satellite pictures.

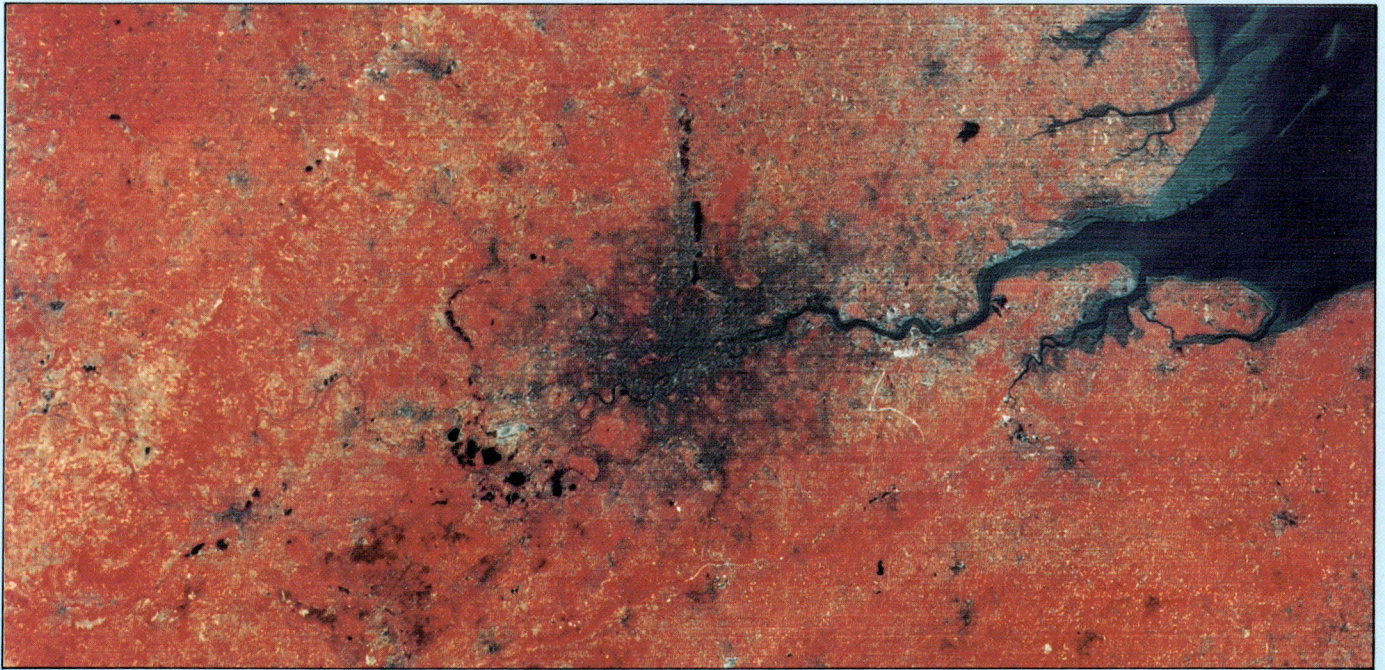

△ A picture of London and the southeast of England, taken by Landsat in infrared light, is shown in false colour. Dark red areas are covered by trees, and lighter red parts are fields. The built-up areas appear grey, and seas and rivers dark blue. The thin white streak to the east of London is a cutting through chalk for a new motorway.

▷ Another false-coloured picture (from a camera on Spacelab) in infrared light shows part of the desert in Sudan. The river is the White Nile, and fields of cotton and millet show up as small dark red squares.

# Glossary

**Aeroshell**  A detachable front cover on a lander that protects it from heat when it enters a planet's atmosphere and slows it down.

**Antenna**  The part of a spacecraft that sends and receives radio messages.

**Asteroid**  One of the many thousands of minor planets, each less than 1,000 km (620 miles) across.

**Astronomy satellite**  A satellite that studies the radiation from distant objects in the Universe.

**Big Bird**  A series of American spy satellites.

**Booster**  A rocket used to launch spacecraft; a "strap-on" booster is a small rocket attached to the side of a larger one, to give extra thrust.

**Cassini**  A planned American-European unmanned spaceprobe to Saturn.

**Comet**  Small icy and dusty body that develops a huge gaseous "head" and long tail when it approaches the Sun.

**Communications satellite**  A satellite used to transmit radio signals around the world: the signals usually carry telephone calls or television broadcasts.

**Direct broadcast satellite**  A satellite that broadcasts television so powerfully that an ordinary person can pick up the signals directly at home.

**Earth resources satellite**  A satellite that observes the Earth to pinpoint reserves of valuable materials, and to monitor the growth of crops, pollution and so on.

**Equatorial orbit**  An orbit above the Earth's equator.

**Flyby**  The passage of a spaceprobe past a body (such as a planet or comet) without stopping to orbit or land on it.

**Galileo**  An American spaceprobe that will orbit the planet Jupiter, and send a small probe into its atmosphere.

**Geostationary orbit**  A circular orbit 35,880 km (22,300 miles) above the Earth's equator. A satellite here seems to hang motionless over the same part of the Earth.

**Giotto**  A European spaceprobe that flew past Halley's Comet in 1986.

**Gravity**  A force that draws every object towards every other object.

**Hotol**  A British design for a spacecraft that flies up and down through the atmosphere like an ordinary plane.

**Hubble Space Telescope**  A telescope that will orbit the Earth: from above the atmosphere, it will have a much clearer view of distant objects.

**Infrared**  A radiation similar to light, but with a longer wavelength.

**Ion drive**  A kind of rocket engine that uses electrical power rather than burning fuel.

**Killer satellite**  A satellite designed to destroy other satellites.

**Lander**  A spacecraft that lands on another world.

**Landsat**  A series of Earth observation satellites.

**Luna**  A series of unmanned Russian spaceprobes to the Moon.

**Lunokhod**  A pair of Russian unmanned vehicles that explored the Moon.

**Mariner**  A series of American spaceprobes that visited Mercury, Venus and Mars.

**Mir**  A Russian space station, launched in 1986.

**Molniya**  A series of Russian communications satellites.

**Navigation satellite**  A satellite that broadcasts radio signals that allow people on Earth to work out their precise position.

**Nucleus**  (of a comet) The small solid object at a comet's centre, made of ice with a dark crust of dust and rock.

**Orbit**  The path of one object around another, under the influence of its gravity.

**Orbiter**  A spacecraft that is in orbit around another world.

**Phobos**  The larger of Mars's two moons; also, a planned Russian unmanned mission to Mars and its moons.

**Pioneer**  A series of American spaceprobes that visited Venus, Jupiter and Saturn.

**Polar orbit**  An orbit that goes over the Earth's poles.

**Radar**  A system which "bounces" radio waves off a target to build up a picture of it.

**Salyut**  A series of Russian space stations.

**Satellite**  An object that is in orbit around another body: often used as a shorthand for "artificial satellite", an object launched from Earth (as opposed to a "natural satellite" such as the Earth's Moon).

**Saturn**  (rocket) A series of powerful American rockets developed to land astronauts on the Moon.

▷ The launch of the Titan/Centaur rocket from Cape Canaveral on 20 August 1977. On board was the Voyager 2 spacecraft, which has since passed Jupiter, Saturn and Uranus and is now heading for Neptune.

**Search and rescue satellite**  A satellite that picks up emergency radio messages from ships and planes and pinpoints the position of the transmitter to guide search parties.

**Solar cell**  A device that converts sunlight into electricity.

**Soyuz**  A series of Russian manned spacecraft.

**Space ark**  A proposed manned spacecraft that would contain hundreds or thousands of people.

**Spaceprobe**  A spacecraft that leaves the Earth's gravity to investigate space beyond.

**Space Shuttle**  A series of manned American spacecraft that are reusable.

**Space station**  A large manned satellite, where people can live for long periods.

**Spot**  A French Earth resources satellite.

**Sputnik**  A series of early unmanned Russian satellites: Sputnik 1, launched in 1957, was the first satellite.

**Spy satellite**  A satellite that takes pictures of military targets on the ground below.

**Star Wars**  An American proposal for a system of satellites that would destroy missiles launched by the enemy during a war (the Strategic Defence Initiative).

# Finding out more

You can use a satellite yourself—simply by making a phone call to another continent! Television weather forecasts also bring satellite pictures into your own home every day. Any display of astronomy will have spaceprobe pictures of the other planets. You can find out more by joining a local or national society.

The main society in the UK for people interested in space is the British Interplanetary Society (27–29 South Lambeth Road, London SW8 1SZ). Beginners may prefer to join the Junior Astronomical Society, whose magazine *Popular Astronomy* also has a section on space: write to Martin Ratcliffe, 36 Fairway, Keyworth, Nottingham NG12 5DU. The British Astronomical Association (Burlington House, Piccadilly, London W1V 9AG) caters for more advanced amateur astronomers: it co-ordinates the serious observation of satellites by amateur astronomers. You might also like to join an astronomical society nearer home: there's a new list of these published each year in Patrick Moore's Yearbook of Astronomy (Sidgwick & Jackson). These societies often have visiting speakers who describe results from satellites and spaceprobes.

There is an extremely good display of satellites, spaceprobes and rockets at the "Exploration of Space" gallery at the Science Museum (Exhibition Road, London SW7). It also has Landsat pictures of London. The Armagh Planetarium, College Hill, Armagh, Northern Ireland, has a good display, weather satellite pictures and an enormous range of spaceprobe pictures that you can call up yourself by computer.

Other places to visit include (check in advance for opening hours): Jodrell Bank Visitor Centre, Macclesfield, Cheshire SK11 9DL; Goonhilly Satellite Earth Station, Helston, Cornwall TR12 6LQ; Museum of Flight, East Fortune, Haddington, East Lothian, Scotland; RAF Aerospace Museum, Cosford, Wolverhampton, West Midlands WV7 3EX.

If you want to know more about different kinds of spacecraft, write to: British Aerospace, PO Box 5, Filton, Bristol BS1 2QW (communications satellites and Giotto); Royal Aircraft Establishment Space Department, Farnborough, Hants GU14 6TD (Earth resources satellites); Meteorological Office, London Road, Bracknell, Berks RG12 2SZ (weather satellites); British National Space Centre, Millbank Tower, Millbank, London SW1P 4QU (general information on UK involvement in space, and on how to become an astronaut).

**Vega**  A pair of unmanned Russian spacecraft that investigated Venus and Halley's Comet.

**Venera**  A series of Russian unmanned spaceprobes to Venus.

**Viking**  A pair of American spaceprobes to Mars in 1976.

**Vostok**  An early series of Russian manned spacecraft: Vostok 1 carried the first person into space in 1961.

**Voyager**  A pair of American unmanned spaceprobes to Jupiter and Saturn; Voyager 2 also passed Uranus, and will reach Neptune in 1989.

**Weather satellite**  A satellite that observes clouds and temperatures.

**Weightlessness**  A feeling of complete lack of weight when in orbit due to the fact that everything in the same orbit is travelling at the same rate.

# Index